Thank you to the generous team who gave their time and talents to make this book possible:

Author
Elizabeth Spor Taylor

Illustrator
April Phillips

Creative Directors
Caroline Kurtz, Jane Kurtz,
and Kenny Rasmussen

Translator
Ahmed Dedo Gemeda

Designer
Beth Crow

Ready Set Go Books, an Open Hearts Big Dreams Project

Special thanks to Ethiopia Reads donors and staff for believing in this project and helping get it started-- and for arranging printing, distribution, and training in Ethiopia.

ISBN: 979-8523546983
Library of Congress Control Number: 2021912688

Published: 06/19/21

Who Am I?

Ani Eenyu?

English and Afaan Oromo

Let's play a game.
Do you know these animals?

Mee tapha tokko taphanna. Bineensota kana beektu?

Who am I?   Ani eenyu?

Here is my black mane.

Kun gaammaa gurraacha kooti.

Can you see my bushy tail?

**Eegee koo yabbuun kun
isinitti mul'ataa?**

I hunt at night.

Galgala nan adamsa.

I am a black-maned lion.

Ani Leenca abbaa gaammaa gurraachaati.

Who am I?   Ani eenyu?

Here are my striped legs.

Miilli koo cocorree kunoo.

Can you see my black eye?

Iji koo gurraachi isinitti mul'ataa?

I eat grass.

Margan sooradha.

I am a Somali wild donkey.

Ani Harree bosonaa Sumaaleeti.

Who am I?   Ani eenyu?

Here is my brown nose.

Funyaan koo halluu magaala qabu kunooti.

Can you see my gray fur?

Haalluun gogaa koo daalachi isinitti mul'ataa.

I live in bamboo trees.

Bosona leemmana keessa jiraadha.

I am a Bale Mountains vervet.

Ani Qamalee gaarreen Baalee ti.

Who am I?   Ani eenyu?

Here are my small ears.

**Gurroonni koo
xixiqqoon kunooti.**

Can you see my pointy nose?

**Huruu funyaan koo
dheeraan isinitti mul'ataa.**

Many people call me a fox.

Namoonni baay'een Jeedala jedhanii na waamu.

I am an Ethiopian wolf.

Ani Yeeyyii Itoophiyaati.

Who am I?   Ani eenyu?

Here is my blue eye.

Iji cuquliisaa koo kunooti.

Can you see my curled tail?

Eegeen koo mammaramaan
isinitti mul'ataa.

I change color.

Halluu koo jijijjiruu nan danda'a.

I am a heather chameleon.

Ani Gaararraadha.

Who am I?　　Ani eenyu?

Here is my yellow head.

Mataan koo keelloo fakkaatu kunooti.

Can you see my green wing?

Koochoon yookaan koolli koo magariisaa isinitti mul'ataa?

I eat fruit.

Fuduraa nan sooradha.

I am a yellow-fronted parrot.

Ani simbirroo mataa keelloo Baqaqaniidha.

Who am I?   Ani eenyu?

Here are my horns.

Gaafni koo kunooti.

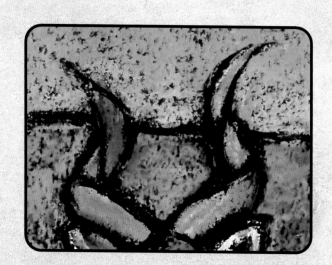

Can you see my striped fur?

Haalluun gogaa koo cocorree isinitti mul'ataa?

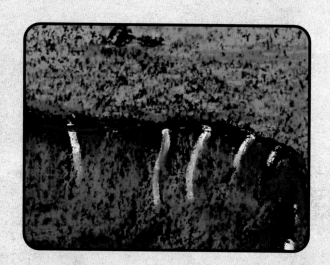

I bark.

Nan iyya.

I am a mountain nyala.

Ani Gadamsa gaaraati.

Who am I?   Ani eenyu?

Here are my white teeth.

Ilkaan koo adiin kunooti.

Can you see my black nose?

Funyaan koo gurraachi
isinitti muldhataa?

I dig tunnels.

Boolla nan qota.

I am a big-headed mole rat.

Ani abbaa mataa guddaa hantuuta
tuqaa jedhamuudha.

Who am I?　　Ani eenyu?

Here is my red chest.

Lapheen koo diimaan kunoo.

Can you see my black eyes?

Iji koo gugurraachi isinitti mul'ataa?

I sleep on cliffs.

Iddoon ciisichaa koo ededa qilee irra.

I am a gelada baboon.

Ani Jaldeessa dha.

Who am I?   Ani eenyu?

Here is my red beak.

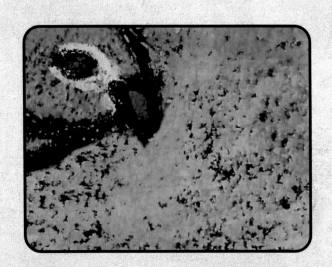

Huruun koo diimaan kunoo.

Can you see my blue tail?

Eegeen koo cuquliisaa isinitti mul'ataa.

I fly from tree to tree.

Mukarraa gara mukaatti nan balali'a.

I am a Prince Ruspoli's Turaco.

Ani ilma mootii Raaspoolis Tarkoodha.

Play again!
Tell your friends about all these amazing animals.

Irraa deebi'aa taphadhaa. Waa'ee bineensota ajaa'iboo kanneen hunda hiriyyoota keessanitti himaa.

About The Story

The animals in this book live only in Ethiopia and nowhere else. One of the most fascinating is the Ethiopian wolf, the rarest wolf in the world and one of only a handful of wolf species in Africa. Many Ethiopians know the animal as the Simien fox. Though it is larger than a fox, there are many characteristics that make it similar. Like a fox, the Ethiopian wolf has red fur, a bushy tail, long legs, a white throat patch, black markings, a long muzzle, and pointed ears. But DNA samples confirm it is directly related to the grey wolf.

Interestingly, Ethiopian wolves and gelada baboons have a symbiotic relationship. Gelada baboons allow Ethiopian wolves to hunt within their herds. When doing so, Ethiopian wolves are twice as likely to capture their prey.

With less than 500 adults alive today, the Ethiopian wolf is the most endangered carnivore in Africa. Since 1995, the Ethiopian Wolf Conservation Programme has collaborated with the Ethiopian government and local communities to protect the Ethiopian wolf. www.ethiopianwolf.org

About The Author

Elizabeth Spor Taylor is an international literacy specialist who served as writer and editor of English learning materials for Ethiopian students. She has traveled to Ethiopia eleven times visiting schools and working collaboratively with Ethiopian educators throughout the country.

Elizabeth became familiar with the successes of Ethiopia Reads while touring sponsored libraries in various regions of Ethiopia. Her expertise is in primary grades literacy relative to native English speakers as well as English Speakers of Other Languages.

She is a contributing member of the Book Centered Learning Committee for Ethiopia Reads and supports the advancement of English skills within the immigrant and refugee population in Cleveland, Ohio.

About the Illustrator

April Phillips' lifelong love for art, both classic and modern, was handed down from her uniquely talented mother. Taking that inspiration, April hopes to inspire another generations' love of art with her book illustrations and teaching.

About Open Hearts Big Dreams

Open Hearts Big Dreams began as a volunteer organization, led by Ellenore Angelidis in Seattle, Washington, to provide sustainable funding and strategic support to Ethiopia Reads, collaborating with Jane Kurtz. OHBD has now grown to be its own nonprofit organization supporting literacy, innovation, and leadership for young people in Ethiopia.

Ellenore Angelidis comes from a family of teachers who believe education is a human right, and opportunity should not depend on your birthplace. And as the adoptive mother of a little girl who was born in Ethiopia and learned to read in the U.S., as well as an aspiring author, she finds the chance to positively impact literacy hugely compelling!

About Ready Set Go Books

Reading has the power to change lives, but many children and adults in Ethiopia cannot read. One reason is that Ethiopia doesn't have enough books in local languages to give people a chance to practice reading. Ready Set Go books wants to close that gap and open a world of ideas and possibilities for kids and their communities.

When you buy a Ready Set Go book, you provide critical funding to create and distribute more books.

Learn more at: http://openheartsbigdreams.org/book-project/

Ready Set Go 10 Books

In 2018, Ready Set Go Books decided to experiment by trying a few new books in larger sizes.

Sometimes it was the art that needed a little more room to really shine. Sometimes the story or nonfiction text was a bit more complicated than the short and simple text used in most of our current early reader books.

We called these our "Ready Set Go 10" books as a way to show these ones are bigger and also sometimes have more words on the page. The response has been great so now our Ready Set Go 10 books are a significant number of our titles. We are happy to hear feedback on these new books and on all our books.

About the Language

The continent of Africa is home to many people who speak Afaan Oromo. Native speakers of Afaan Oromo, in fact, outnumber speakers of every other language except Arabic, Swahili and Hausa. Most Afaan Oromo speakers live in Ethiopia. (Many also live in the United States.) Using the Latin alphabet for writing Afaan Oromo can be traced back to the nineteenth century but was formally adopted in 1991.

About the Translation

Ahmed Dedo Gemeda is an Assistant Professor of English Language and Literature at Haramaya University. He is currently teaching undergraduate and postgraduate students. He is also serving as a translator, editor and reviewer on academic, technical and literary works.

Over 100 unique Ready Set Go books available!

 To view all available titles, search "Ready Set Go Ethiopia" or scan QR code

 Chaos

 Talk Talk Turtle

 The Glory of Gondar

 We Can Stop the Lion

 Not Ready!

 Fifty Lemons

 Count For Me

 Too Brave

 Tell Me What You Hear

Open Heart Big Dreams is pleased to offer discounts for bulk orders, educators and organizations.

Contact ellenore@openheartsbigdreams.org for more information.

Made in the USA
Middletown, DE
07 January 2023

21528000R00020